The REAL Three Little PIGS

– as told by the big (not bad) wolf

Kristina Spieker

Write and Release
PUBLISHING

www.writeandreleasepublishing.com

Hi! My name is Walter...Walter Wolf. You may have heard people refer to me as, "The Big Bad Wolf." Let me just say, it was all a big misunderstanding, and it looked a lot worse than it was.

Everyone is usually scared of wolves, so I was quite lonely until I moved here to Sunny Lane. My new neighbors were so welcoming – and now we are the best of friends!

Perry, Patrick, and Paxton are great pigs to hang out with. They made their houses all by themselves. Can you believe it? I had to have my mom help me build my house.

Those three pigs are so similar. They love to play games, be outside and race each other. But when it came to making their houses, they could not be more different.

Perry built his house out of straw. He likes the way it feels. The straw is scratchy and he loves having a good itch.

Patrick made his house out of sticks because he is a musician and likes the sound to travel throughout the neighborhood. He also likes to feel the cool breeze as it passes through the gaps.

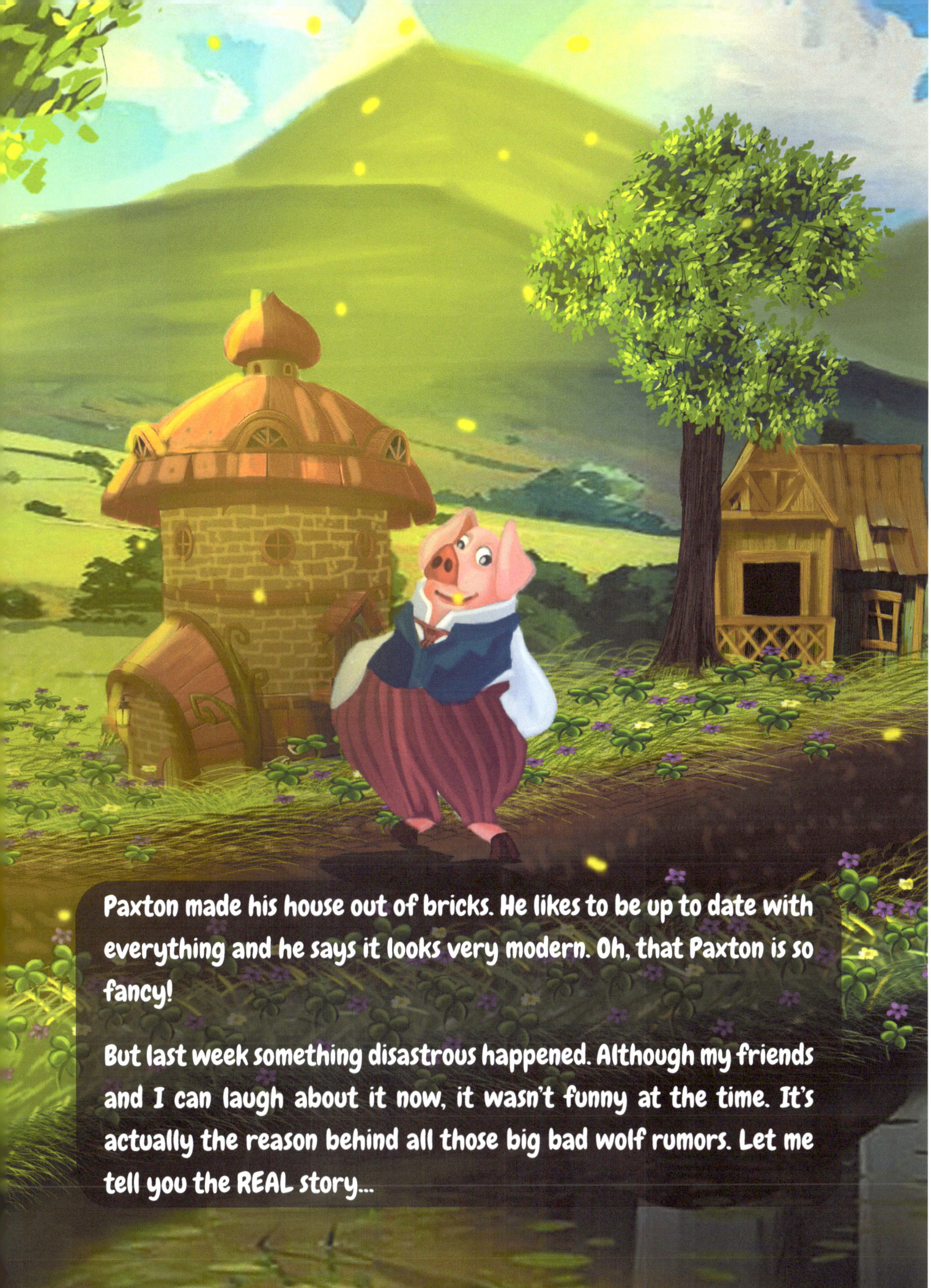

Paxton made his house out of bricks. He likes to be up to date with everything and he says it looks very modern. Oh, that Paxton is so fancy!

But last week something disastrous happened. Although my friends and I can laugh about it now, it wasn't funny at the time. It's actually the reason behind all those big bad wolf rumors. Let me tell you the REAL story...

I was in the mood for some chocolate chip cookies, so I decided to make a batch. I was so eager to start eating that when the timer went off I reached into the oven and grabbed the cookie sheet – without my oven mitt!

"YEEE-ouch!" I yelled, burning my paw. As you know, a burn needs ice, but I didn't have any. So I ran over to Perry's house – I was sure he'd have some!

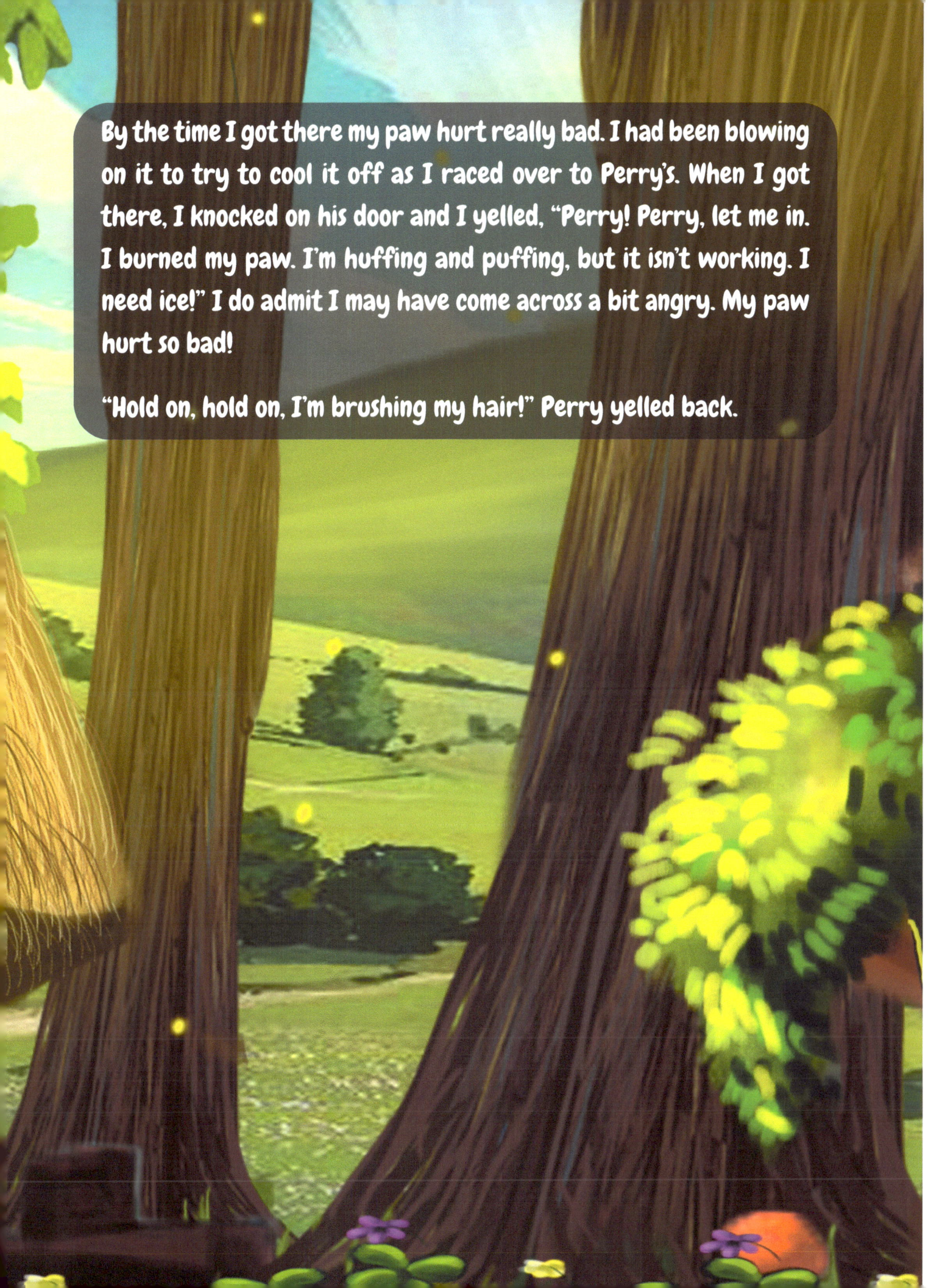

By the time I got there my paw hurt really bad. I had been blowing on it to try to cool it off as I raced over to Perry's. When I got there, I knocked on his door and I yelled, "Perry! Perry, let me in. I burned my paw. I'm huffing and puffing, but it isn't working. I need ice!" I do admit I may have come across a bit angry. My paw hurt so bad!

"Hold on, hold on, I'm brushing my hair!" Perry yelled back.

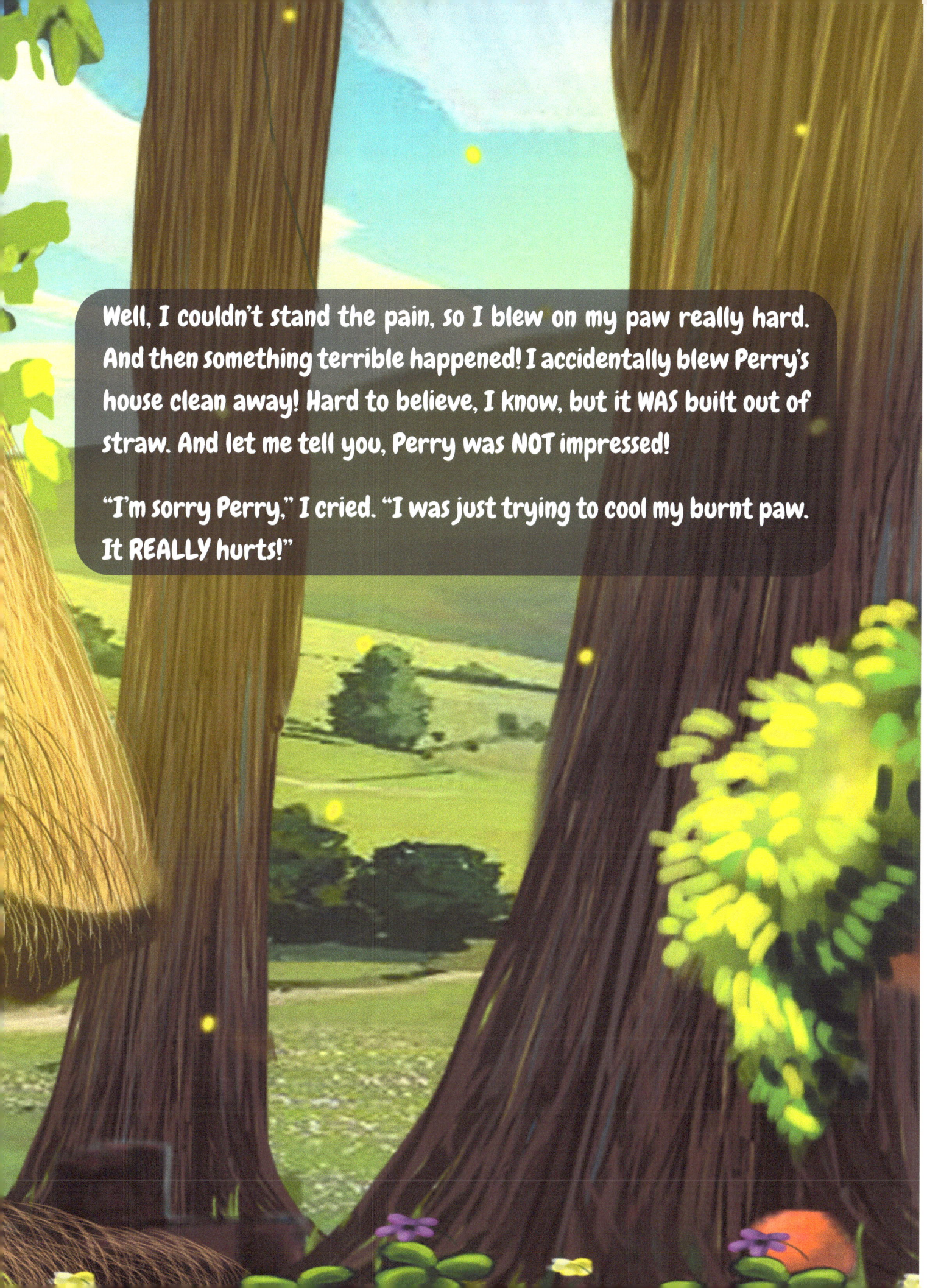

Well, I couldn't stand the pain, so I blew on my paw really hard. And then something terrible happened! I accidentally blew Perry's house clean away! Hard to believe, I know, but it WAS built out of straw. And let me tell you, Perry was NOT impressed!

"I'm sorry Perry," I cried. "I was just trying to cool my burnt paw. It REALLY hurts!"

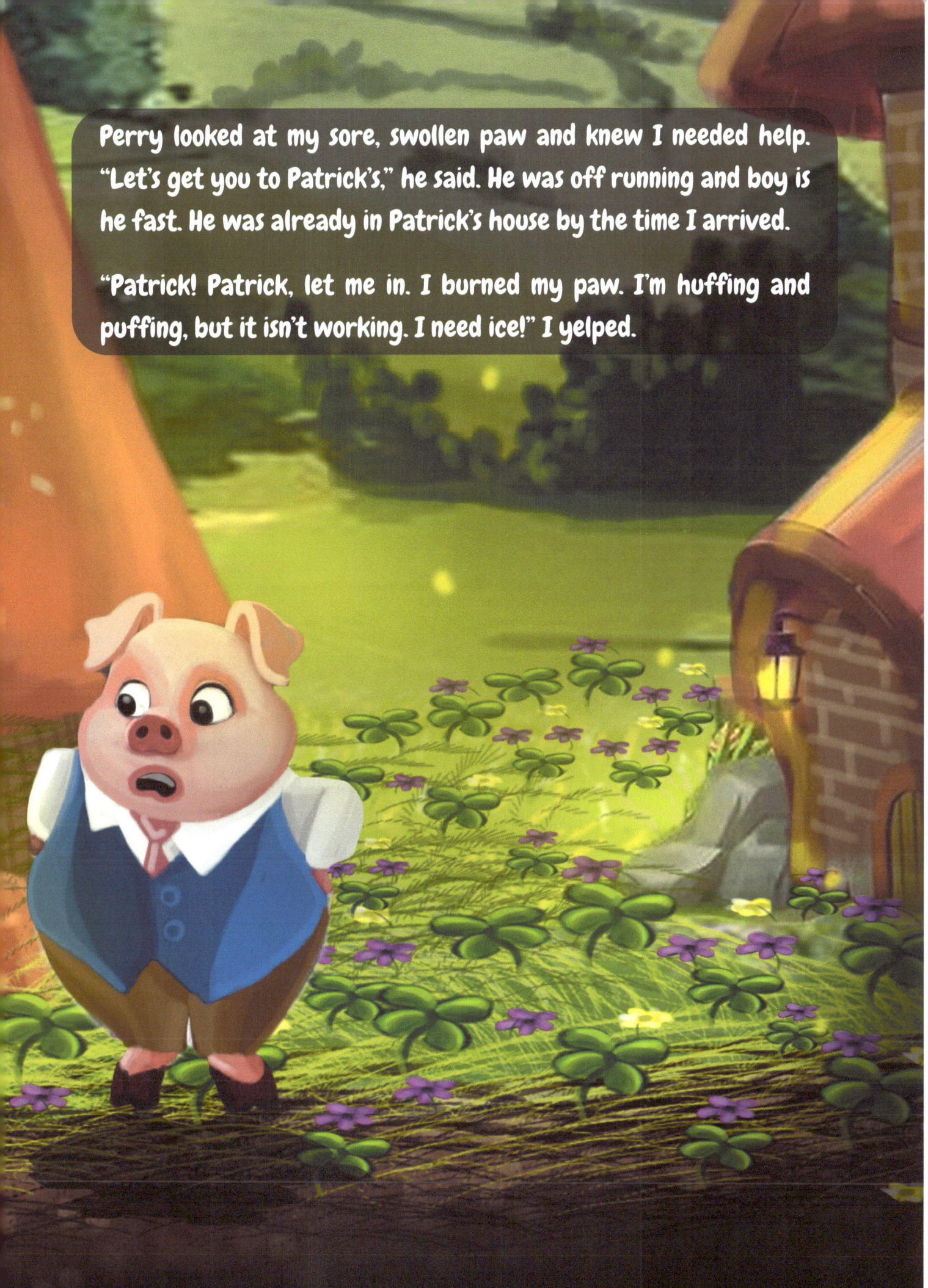

Perry looked at my sore, swollen paw and knew I needed help. "Let's get you to Patrick's," he said. He was off running and boy is he fast. He was already in Patrick's house by the time I arrived.

"Patrick! Patrick, let me in. I burned my paw. I'm huffing and puffing, but it isn't working. I need ice!" I yelped.

There was a lot of commotion inside Patrick's house. He had been playing music all morning and his instruments must have been laying all over. It sounded like Perry knocked some over on his way in the door. I could hear Perry saying, "He needs ice. Hurry, he needs ice."

And Patrick yelled back, "What? He isn't being nice?"

"No...ICE!" Perry yelled. "HE NEEDS ICE!"

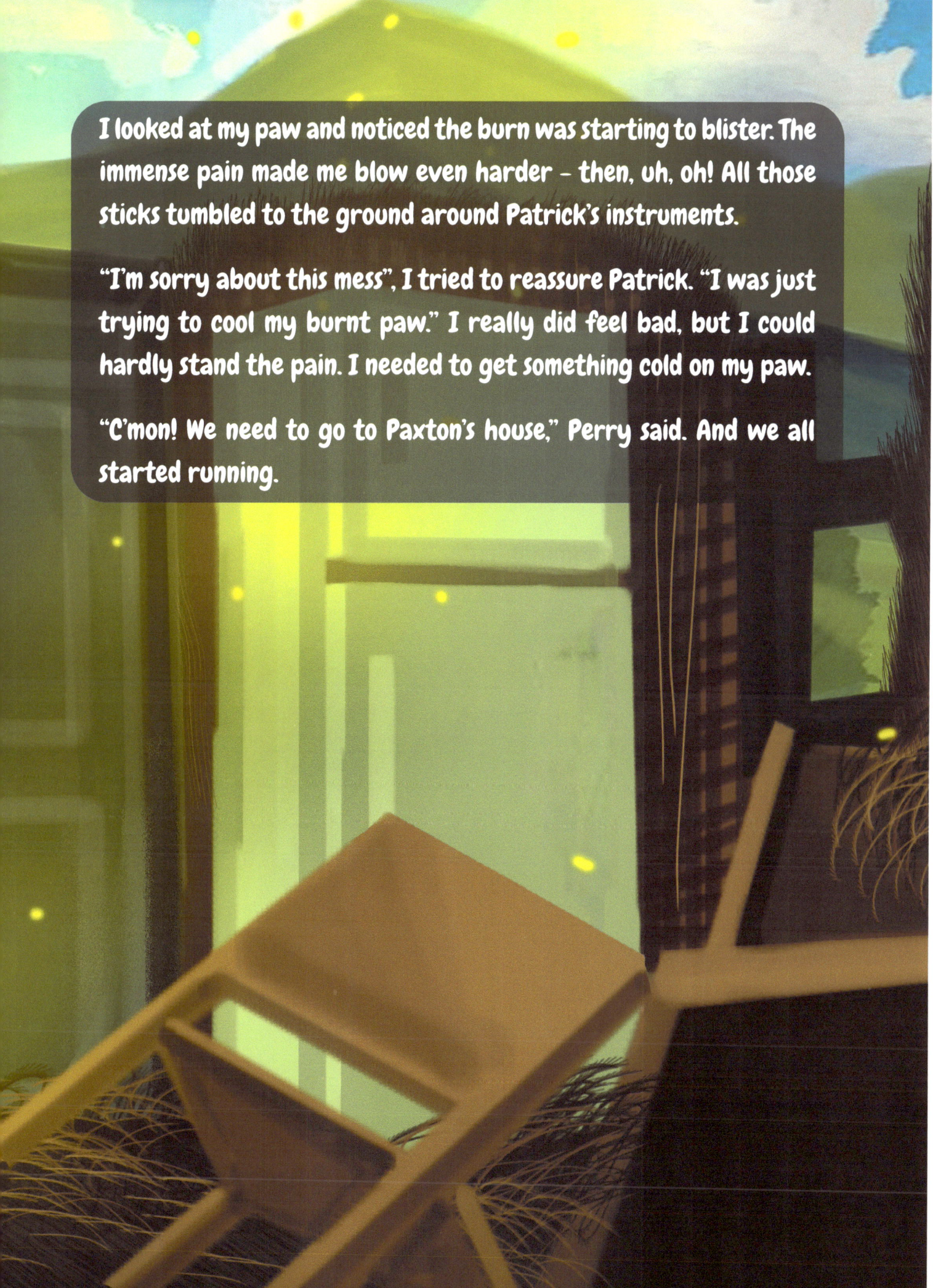

I looked at my paw and noticed the burn was starting to blister. The immense pain made me blow even harder – then, uh, oh! All those sticks tumbled to the ground around Patrick's instruments.

"I'm sorry about this mess", I tried to reassure Patrick. "I was just trying to cool my burnt paw." I really did feel bad, but I could hardly stand the pain. I needed to get something cold on my paw.

"C'mon! We need to go to Paxton's house," Perry said. And we all started running.

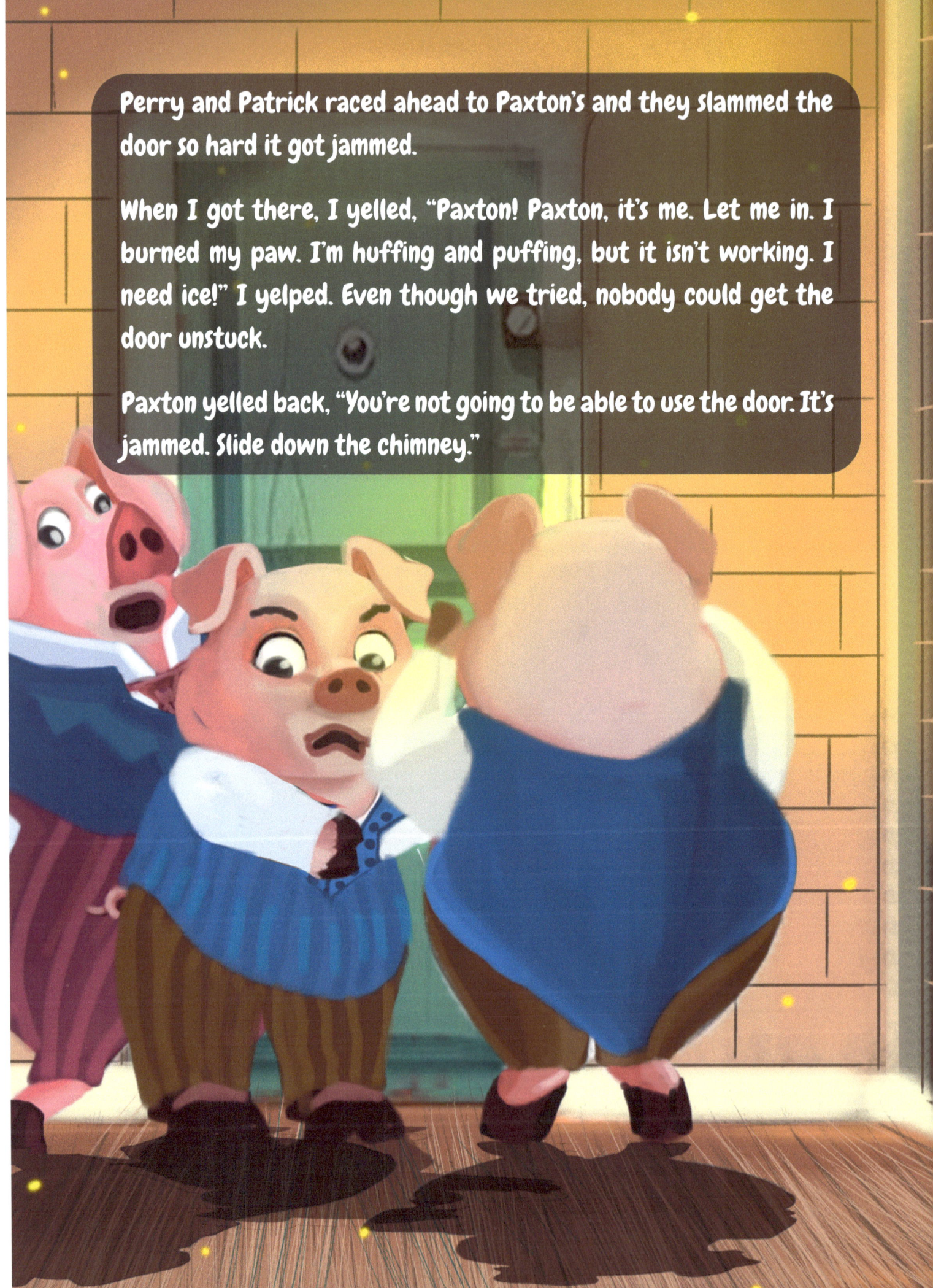

Perry and Patrick raced ahead to Paxton's and they slammed the door so hard it got jammed.

When I got there, I yelled, "Paxton! Paxton, it's me. Let me in. I burned my paw. I'm huffing and puffing, but it isn't working. I need ice!" I yelped. Even though we tried, nobody could get the door unstuck.

Paxton yelled back, "You're not going to be able to use the door. It's jammed. Slide down the chimney."

Well, I thought that was a crazy idea. I pondered how I would just slide down a chimney. I would have to climb onto the roof just to get to it. And what if I got stuck?

I was desperate to relieve my throbbing paw and I could see no other way inside, so I took a deep breath and found a tree nearby to climb. From there I jumped to the roof of Paxton's house. I ran to the chimney, and without thinking jumped in and slid down. "YYYOOOOUCH!" I yelled as I landed on the floor with a thud.

I immediately ran to Paxton's freezer and plunged my paw inside. "Ah! Relief at last!" I said as Perry and Patrick rushed over to see if I was okay.

"Yum! Something smells good," I said.

"I'm making soup. You guys can stay for supper," Paxton replied.

"Thanks!" We all responded.

As we dished up our soup Patrick asked, "Now what are we going to do about our houses?" And we all started laughing. What a fiasco! All for some ice!

At that point, I realized I was quite hungry and Paxton's soup looked delicious, but it was quite hot. As I started to blow on it to cool it down, all three pigs gave me a very concerned look.